Not Xanadu

This brilliant and absorbing collection of poems, Cathryn Hankla's tenth, greets us with "not," refusing a poetic paradise; and goes on to embrace trees, birds, stars, American history, and the ghosts of roses. Craft and feeling intensify each other throughout; especially in the Cinquain Sonnets and their lightning, rough-edged resolutions. The past is adamant. To articulate its refusals disturbs memory, muddies, and clarifies. Undeceived, mind and heart must somehow adjust. Experience stands half-built and half-demolished, vulnerable, "Not Xanadu." That is this book's challenge and its radiance.

—Angela Ball

The poems in Cathryn Hankla's *Not Xanadu* are clear-eyed and sharp-tongued, vulnerable, unabashed, and prescient. To live in our moment, they suggest, we'd best be alert to absurdity as well as beauty, and hold close moments of reverie as well as face affronts—to know both "the broken egg and the living bird." A close observer of both nature and the use and misuse of language, a runner, a native Appalachian, a mindful woman, Hankla can suggest volumes in the merest phrase. From "Four-Chambered Heart," a love letter to a ruffed grouse, to "Mr. Liberty," composed of passages from Patrick Henry's still inspiring speeches, these lyric and keen poems have in equal measure seriousness of purpose and lightness of touch.

—Carol Moldaw

Not Xanadu's poems make an indispensable *contribution to the subject they/were subject to;* many subjects: despair, broken-heartedness, regret, bitterness, careful observation of one's self and what one sees, awe, hope and how *the soul searches its identities,* with what might be *impossible/in this world, but maybe not in the next.* Hankla's written a book that lets us see why poems are written. The poem "Considering the Alternative" shows the way.

—Dara Wier

By Cathryn Hankla

POETRY

Phenomena
Afterimages
Negative History
Texas School Book Depository
Poems for the Pardoned
Emerald City Blues
Last Exposures
Great Bear
Galaxies
Not Xanadu

FICTION

Learning the Mother Tongue
A Blue Moon in Poorwater
The Land Between
Fortune Teller Miracle Fish

NONFICTION

Lost Places: On Losing and Finding Home

Not Xanadu

poems

Cathryn Hankla

Cathy Hankla

for Margaret ♥
15 years +
much love, Cathy

MERCER UNIVERSITY PRESS
Macon, Georgia

MUP/ H1022

© 2022 by Cathryn Hankla
Published by Mercer University Press
1501 Mercer University Drive
Macon, Georgia 31207

25 24 23 22 21   5 4 3 2 1

Printed and bound in CANADA.

This book is set in Adobe Caslon Pro.

Cover/jacket design by Burt&Burt.

ISBN   978-0-88146-832-8
Cataloging-in-Publication Data is available from the Library of Congress

CONTENTS

My days are swifter than a runner;
they flee away; they see no good.
They go by like skiffs of reed,
like an eagle swooping on the prey.

Job 9: 25–26

The race is not to the swift
or the battle to the strong,
nor does food come to the wise
or wealth to the brilliant
or favor to the learned;
but time and chance happen to them all.

Ecclesiastes 9:11

MERCER UNIVERSITY PRESS

Endowed by

TOM WATSON BROWN
and
THE WATSON-BROWN FOUNDATION, INC.

Not Xanadu

IF I AM WRONG

You don't want this poem.
If I am wrong, then stop

writing the other poem in your head
as you read. I heard one

on the radio—terrible—couldn't
wait for it to be done,

but in my head as it droned on—
a more perfect poem.

If that poem said *stick figures*,
my poem said *stuck no more*.

If that poem said *apricot* or *Massachu-
setts*, my poem said *Croatoan* or

sea otter. When that poem said,
Sometimes my microwave beeps

a dire warning, this poem said,
The odd whistles of which you've been

complaining issue from my African Grey.
When the elevator doors opened

in that poem, on an unfamiliar floor,
strangers waved an important piece of

my mail. *We would have gotten
this back to you sooner*, that poem said,

But we were on a Caribbean cruise, and
our family members drank too much.

As you know, we don't drink.
In this poem, we take the stairs,

my statement's delivered on time, and
I rewrite the end over and over.

RUNNER

Dear local Mountie,
Please don't arrest me,
though it may seem only the guilty flee.

Sure, I pick up the pace when passing
the homeless man staked
beneath the bridge amassing

testaments in scrap tin,
a neighbor's straining lab
who "won't hurt you," or the bin

of burgeoning refuse.
But of me let it be said, I'd march
ten miles in a snowstorm scatting blues

just to avoid my strangulation
whenever I must
see a certain person and bar mention

of a decade spent. Perhaps
I'm slower than most to move on
or just one of love's timeless saps,

though my object be impervious,
retaining no sign
of tender feelings previous.

She's my one-armed killer of commitment,
and I'm a *Fugitive* redux:
I'll stop when I find the real culprit.

A TREE

Her half-covered face, a wound
garden hose ready to strike.
Rough over rough, cloth conceals

her skin. Engines dim, the pigeons
chirr and whimper. Umbrellas shade
and hold the sun. The woman's

legs curve uselessly. Eye sealed
with a scar. A blood orange
lush on a tree of no harvest.

AUTOETHNOGRAPHY: ROSES

1.
Please, please
be less pale, I plead
my case to myself—
the boy's vigil
on the stoop,
my father's furious
gurgling at the boy—then
a man's voice on the phone,

cords blistered
from a Brooklyn parsonage,
says he's finally gotten over me.
We're both past forty—
my father's stone dead,
buried with his old-school purities.

2.
You sound funny,
little Appalachian girl,
like you're not that bright
and prob-ly a hillbilly
from up a holler or stranger
than— You sound dumb,
bet you can't play chess,
looks like you're going

to be paid less for working harder,
70 cents on the dollar.
A Black teen who studied Greek
still waits on the doorstep,
a dozen roses and thorns
rustling waxed green paper.

CINQUAIN SONNETS

THOU SHALT NOT

Before the falling taut, the blast. And next
the fire with human hands collects a kill
and offers meat to test what strength I've saved—
pinned butterflies inside until the end—
I know the flesh unblessed. But reach to eat.

I CAN'T

Fingers gnawing toward a lie find brittle
stems still nimble. Layers of mountain green
my eye, blue on blue, flowering into
hills, a last canopy as cirrus trill,
erasing themselves. I can't be a cloud.

FIGHT/FLIGHT/FREEZE

I kept my fingers tight inside my ears
to keep their fight outside my head. Smoking,
drunken, they'd swear. Swaddled in ghostly light,
I'd sweat in blankets summer nights, seeking
my place, a quiet, dark circumference.

WHIRLIGIG

I watch a maple whirlybird twirl by
miracle and muscle. Five times I've brought
the future on too soon or held the past
too long. Samaras, tree helicopters
pelt me. I hold my breath and tigers bloom.

PARADISE ISLAND

The sun returns unchanged. Coconuts drop
or circumvent, but you are different.
Tourists squawk, parrots talk, and my question
waits unattended. Straw, jitneys, and conch—
you decide to wander. I shop and shop.

HONEYMOON

Night reprieves the shore, and lovers struggle
to see stars through muggy air, Jupiter
bright, brighter than Betelgeuse ever was.
Afterward, the sky receded from us.
Once home again, we flattened specimens.

DIVINING

Wind twists old sweetgums, global ornate seed
pods, fierce symmetries with S's for stems.
What is it about regret's swift ambush?
A split of branches divines water's seam.
I walk behind the rod, remembering.

HEAVY DOOR

The rustic door scraped across the marble floor, and beyond the foyer she could see nothing. Feeling for a light switch and failing to find one, she pushed the wooden door closed with both hands. She inched forward until her sandal met the first step. Taking the next step and the next, she patted the wall, still searching, until a larger space, a landing, presented itself.

Stairs turned in new directions, and she climbed without a modicum of light. The fault must be with her eyes, her rods or was it cones not making proper adjustments. Every darkness is a portal, she thought.

Five flights up, after missing the lock several times, at last her key fit and she stepped inside her rented loft. A bit of indirect light and indecipherable music, refracted through the window from the central shaft, led to a small liquid square of night, yet not one star.

DIVERSION

The acrid odor of green walnut husks—
snakes rustle leaves chasing patchy sunlight—
a musk like fish bellies thudding the grass,
Osage Orange shedding slick ghoulish brains.

Skunks wobble through these nights, messy as dreams.
Opossum tiptoes the fence not toppling
and turns his solemn face seeking mercy.
All up to me to let this creature be.

Wind changes direction on whim and nerve—
my fire will cinder eventually.
My father wrecked his car in October
while Mother's hand was declared the dummy.

October's sirens brought November's wake.
Memories of those lost return and ache.

THE RAVISHING

Christian mystics wrote of this,
the seizure that pours
from an opening shining toward
Mystery, poised for the Holy wafer.

A darter can be a diving bird,
or it can swim freshwater as a fish:
the soul searches its moorings
in angels or heretics.

Wandering the grass barefoot,
I stumble on rock, brush earth
and wind-tossed leaves from a marker
for the nameless unremembered.

ROANOKE LOGPERCH

King of the darters, your small body spans no more than
the length of my hand. Dancing fins splay along your spine
fanning coyly. Fancy feathered head dresses undulate as you,
insectivorous, shift clear waters, nosing gravels.
Narrow body tinted green, rimmed red at times
and slashed with generous tiger darkness,
someone transposed you into a public tank
where you sloshed until perishing.
Painting your lightening belly, I reach for yellow to distinguish
you from splashes startling your habitat.

TO MAKE A COLLAGE

Lifted from context and pasted,
nothing will be recognizable

as either invasive or native. Colors
and shapes align or overlap,

alternating large and small,
jagged and smooth, with rich

intensity to juxtapose poor
blurry hints of flower or flesh.

This bit of iridescence pared
by an exacto blade, a flash

of indigo bunting, abuts
the plum snippet from

a model's cashmere cloak.
Beside green blueberries

lost in their immature bush,
a bluebird, excised from his

field, struggles across space,
swims against a skyscraper's

repetitious mirrors,
the suggestion of a glacier.

CONSIDERING THE ALTERNATIVE

Not much of an endorsement
for starters. He got the one who was not

nearly as dumb as the others. The one not half
as plump nor a quarter as conservative.

It was dark, but it could have been worse.
He could have been taller than she

remembered, his face half-obscured
by daylight streaking in from the street,

but she could see him, albeit not
perfectly. Their rock-strewn path—

what mountain trail is not—zigzagged,
but it could have been muddy and wasn't,

which is not to say they could not
have used more sunlight on every subject,

especially when he said he'd be back
in August, and her voice froze, wheels

spinning. She forgot to utter the first word
about her leaving in September. But

at any rate, they made it through, while
not exactly tackling the hour like pros,

they made a contribution to the subject they
were subject to, and might I also venture

to say they executed better than expected
given the odds, since they had such a low bar

to shimmy, owing not to this very moment
nor to any foul or flag on the present play, but

to separate, relatively equal past failures,
encompassing each other not a whit. To wit,

she got to say she was not a needy person,
and he got to ask his first pointed question,

as odd as it was to hear, when her major
dispositional downside had always been

independence or too much of it, and not even
trying, as someone said, to fit in. At any rate,

her fault inflated her for once; it's all about
context, strengths and weaknesses aside,

which is to say this sentence could not
be more meaningless. Unless he wraps

his arms around her and feels something
inside other than regret, obligation, or

a form of childhood angst, it ain't happening.
In other words, awakening's the trick,

and it's going to take more than this here
poem. But we're pulling for them, whoever

we are. We watched the game, someone
had to sit this one out, and we cheered,

which is not to say we were ambivalent
exactly. We wore the right colors, or

at some point we had had the experience
of rooting sincerely for the home team

at another's expense. For my part, I even
marched in the band, performing synchronized

maneuvers at halftime with my clarinet.
Beneath their more or less composed exteriors

they were not really quaking, after all
they are adults, but they could have been

if they had been attuned, if they had known
what we now know. I've heard it said

that no one gets out of here alive, and although
she didn't dodge his final question—what

brand of cynicism is that, I'm not really
asking. Well, I heard one got out alive, and

they called a draw, faked in opposite directions
for extra yardage, whereupon his mother

and children mushroomed at her feet. This
cannot happen that often, she started thinking.

And then I remembered Buster Keaton's
saying in his autobiography that it was about

timing—and keeping a straight face,
someone added—how he was sucked

from his crib into the mouth of a twister,
carried most of a mile and plunked

up a tree. And in a minute or two
she heard his mother's phone ringing.

I'm talking to Cathy, his mother told him.
All or part of this might be true.

RUNNER, CROWS

Three strays guard the sidewalk
spaced like sphinxes
as I huff.

Nothing more startling than
a paw might extend, but
that is doubtful.

A Black man pulling his patched
sedan up to the curb catches
my eye for the nod.

Painters check and climb ladders,
carrying their first buckets
to the eaves.

Driving a red scooter, a young
pale woman swerves me
on the narrow bridge.

Below the bridge, five lanes
of coal cars wait to sparkle
as the sun ascends.

Above the bridge, sentinel crows
purchase the lamppost, cawing
a warning or blessing.

PSALM BIRDS

1.
Like a bird alone on a housetop,
I sang of the flooded valley,
beseeching my best love
with winter coming on, two
yellow birds small as ornaments
on my palm, swift hearts like mine
stinging with power. Our Fraser firs
held song birds frozen in silver glass.
I clipped them on branches
as if the solstice tree were still alive
on an Appalachian mountainside,
as if mountains were abiding.

2.
Like an owl among the ruins
from the roof of a downtown building,
not the limestone outcrop that once
was home, I surveyed the center
of the alley. I caught my fill, swooping
while others slept. In daylight,
I kept to my perch. Then came a man
to roost. Rifles discharged rounds,
scattering flocks that never bothered
me, but shat on cars as city starlings
must. I flew for a day and a night
and never found my cliffs. I flew
above the frothing sea. Above
me, trails of plasma sparked.

FOUR-CHAMBERED HEART

Ruffed grouse, the longing in our four-chambered hearts
was matched when you fluttered toward me as I sat,

beer in hand, on my deck. At first, I didn't get it.
You rounded my chair, dark collar and mottled tail imploring,

flexing, a banty dancer in fringed leggings and mask.
Circumnavigating, fanned tail waving its coal band—

or butterflies or a waterfall—puffy neck a black planet,
you drew closer, for reasons I did not understand.

I thought my ribs quaked over nothing, but you thrummed
for me, secreted in brush, and came a-courting.

The second day, your wings pulsed from my porch railings,
rising in volume and complexity, finally blurring

into love's purring engine. Hopping down to circle
my chair with practiced artistry, you hoisted your tail full sail—

my astonishment almost complete. On the third day
of your strutting display, worry turned me sullen.

You obsessed, proud crest erect. I knew I had to go away,
leave you for weeks. I prayed you'd find, in my absence,

a perfect mate. You argued, a-flutter and dipping and awhirl.
I tried to work it through as you entreated and swayed

alone, almost flying at me, swerving out of tune
before crashing back into wobbly orbit. Was I not moved

by such ardor? I hope you found her, yet I wait for
your return. I'll never forget you, ruffed grouse, or

your persistent drumming after what's impossible
in this world, but maybe not, in the next.

MY TREASURE

My feet find uneven ground shaved to dust by the blade.
Complete and bearable, my ache,
heart balanced on the scale.
My life, the broken egg and the living bird:
a blue jay feather is my treasure.

DEAR SYLVIA

I wait for you here with my coffee cup
and newspaper, and I watch the sea.

The dolphins head up the beach
and in the evening scallop down.

The force of their numbers through surf
pushes toward the condo village,

past gnashing mongrels gathered
on shore. The dogs collect every morning

to stalk grackles, whose molting feathers
stick out like charred trash or timbers.

Even if these grackles were crash sites,
only dogs would investigate.

Sylvia, I watch the dolphins skimming by
undulating, their splendid continuum

unbroken, water like silk shedding from
their slick gray backs.

Sylvia, I am still waiting for you
to notice—turn toward my shining skin.

IN THE GARDEN

Tomatoes cling to withering
vines, outpacing split skins and chill.

At the end of the Republic
some voices are heard and some not.

Hasn't it always been like this,
your body only a seed pod

for what lies ahead? As Jesus
said, I will, like Jonah, arise.

They came, weeping, to tend his crypt.
He visited two Marys first.

I go out into my garden,
what's left of it giving last shrugs,

seeking now just powdery leaves,
places where the light might linger.

RUNNING COMMENTARY

COAL TRAIN

Overshadowed by engine 8157,
hounding the historic rail walk
I am not bound for heaven.

Neither am I every woman—
it goes without saying—
when to prefix man

with *wo* indicates non-
standard, questionable, in
other words, *nothing like the sun.*

I jog past heavily tagged cars
loaded with deep pit coal
that glitters like negative stars.

Hero's journey, quest pattern,
this is not that, ad infinitum.

BEES KNEES

Though of woe born, I am no thug.
I do take issue with the questions
swept beneath my rug.

But no hugs, please, they only
serve to stir my caldron,
bless my heart & buzz my bonnet's bees.

You tighten the twitch around
my tender muzzle as you irrigate
the blooming wound,

commanding my hobbled hoofs
be still. Do what you will
in the name of healing. Raise the roof

if you must. I once fell at your feet—
pledged forever, best friend & help meet.

MY SPARROW

Abrupt break-my-reverie sparrow,
I step over you, dank bird with no blood,
victim felled by invisible blows

that decimate yet leave no trace.
Look to cumulonimbus clouds,
chiaroscuro balancing my face,

& can you, having flown, name
their strata? I draw a blank.
You taught me how to tame

my inner hurricane & for your
sake I strangled not to blurt
the brooding questions that tore

a path from gut to this tired world,
seeking answers forever untold.

CURED

It felt like the world
turned upside down & inside out,
besieged by a medieval sword

piercing silence despite
several lies unearthed—
your claims on crest & rights

restored. No doubt
my failure at repression helped.
Yet speaking truth had no clout

in our boudoir.
A tie can be many times cut
& mended before

its final rend. The puny bird
is resting now & quite cured.

REVERIE

Three ladies in slick bee hives
are my loves supreme.
They sway the smooth hip,

tip a gesture to the sky.
Where did our love go?
Burning, yearning, turning, hurts.

You don't owe me the rest of—
like silk in a knot,
ohh, baby, baby—your life.

TRANSMOGRIFY

Some claim Lady Gaga used to be a tiny baby,
some claim she used to be a housefly

on the wall of witness. Follow the <u>link</u>.
In the baby there rose a cry that grew into

Rapunzel-like, unbelievably strong woven locks,
or branches of a fatally flawed tree.

Legends are for undying. All unlawful citizens
were at one time scared. Their terror turned

into terrifying. The trinkets of humanity
jingle as they walk. No one is supposed

to guess they bear resemblance:
the uniformed and the man arrested.

AWFUL PROJECT

The tank rolled toward my house,
reaching an impossible height.
It drew closer and parked—
a tiny man climbed out.

Reaching an impossible height—
my roof peak rose no taller—
a tiny man climbed out
who tumbled several stories.

My roof peak rose no taller
than war, misery, or the soldier
who tumbled several stories,
to land upright on military boots.

Than war, misery, or the soldier,
there is no more awful project.
To land upright on military boots
is to find a certain order.

There is no more awful project,
I presumed, but wrongly,
than to find a certain order.
Tiny man stormed my kitchen,

I presumed, but wrongly,
to find someone to murder.
Tiny man stormed my kitchen
in his boots, toting loafers.

>

To find something to murder
him with, I rummaged cabinets.
In his boots, toting loafers,
tiny man sat down to change.

MR. LIBERTY: Selected Passages from Patrick Henry

March 23, 1775, Second Revolutionary Convention

This is no time for ceremony—

Should I keep back my opinions
at such a time, through fear of giving offense,
I should consider myself as guilty of treason

towards my country, and of an act of disloyalty
toward the Majesty of Heaven,
which I revere above all earthly

kings....Shall we acquire the means
of effectual resistance by lying supinely
on our backs and hugging the delusive

phantom of hope, until our enemies
shall have bound us hand and foot?
We are apt to shut our eyes

against a painful truth, and listen
to the song of that siren
till she transforms us into beasts....

Let us not deceive ourselves, sir.

WHAT ARE THE CHANCES

What we know now
Evidently
Your best bet
However
Going forward

Deep discounts
Reach out
Limited time offer
Touch base
Individually wrapped

Double back
Relieved to hear
Believed to be true
Not under warranty
Without a doubt

Having said that
In the long run
After a fashion
At any rate
I cannot recall

EVERYMAN

Neither bootlicker nor boot blacker,
not a message in a bottle, nor bottled up,
nor a blocker of missives sent.
In short and in brief, in holus-bolus
fullness, he was.

Clay pigeons burst forth from a canon,
and rounds erupted to pierce his
thin travail. He cradled a smoky taper,
melted wax bleeding onto

the paper guarding his hand.
With a sable brush, he crossed out
a number of misguided letters
in a number of words he was writing.

In the pincushion universe,
marching in a periodic sentence, losing
his parallelism at Wounded Knee, he fell
on a sword of agreements. He died and
arose, and ever he was....

NO MATCH

I said, no bluster, "Friends first."
His paragraph about himself

began with "Work...." That's
promising, I thought, but in as much

as we are poised to discuss imminent
exchanges of body stuff, our

lives beyond this steamy car lack
relevance. He paws

my hair as I drive us here and there,
straining not to blurt,

"Stop it, Buster!" Arms plastered
to my sides by his hug,

I seal my lips against a plunging
tongue, my neckline bundled,

breasts as if bound. Repeating
junior high, we are doomed.

Fancy font on his t-shirt says,
"Beaver Canoe."

AUTOETHNOGRAPHY: FIRST JOB BLUES

Sixteen in the stockroom,
pinned on the ladder
by the boss for a kiss.

"This won't be the last time
some man tries, and
sometime you'll say yes."

ONION STORY

1.
The sharpest knife
is not of metal.

2.
She wants to marry
Red Onion.

3.
So many tears,
salves and haints:
this time's no different

from Peer Gynt's scene
of peeling
and sobbing.

4.
Part her like
a Red Sea.

Cross her.

5.
When her body gives out,
bury her sprouts of green.

She'll live again.

WHAT'S COOKING

Reading a stranger's obituary, I think of the many conventions she had in her life as insurance against despair: husband, children, grandchildren. But things are not as they appear. Yesterday, my mother showed me her daily Bible verse: "We fix our eyes not on what is seen but on what is unseen." One of her favorites, she said. I suppose she got a lot of practice in that trick by living with my dad. And while I have been writing, the oatmeal boiled over on the stove. This is how it is for us, back and forth, back and forth. The pot on the stove, the living.

WASHING MOTHER'S CLOTHES
FOR THE LAST TIME

The rinse cycle spins tangled intimates
like straw that must be spun night after night
into gold, her silk pajamas, my whale
hump bras breaching with camisoles and socks,
yellowed slips, abandoned feminine props.
In her final years all the primping stopped.
I polish her glasses as if she needs
to see. I don't know if she sees me here,

still trying to do anything I can
to interrupt the natural cycle
with a wager of care. I was never
the perfect daughter she treated me as:
my charms, ring, and labor traded for days.
Mother's wet clothes and mine wring together.

CAN YOU DRAW OUT A LEVIATHAN
WITH A FISHHOOK?

My mother left her blood
in her Bible,
spilled from agèd hands
like wine from old vines.

It stained the Book of Job
when God's talking.
Most of the blood smear
covers *for ever*.

Dab a drop of water,
and a sermon
washes over me—
how little I know.

IT MUST BE

Terrible not to quake
when love enters the room,
not to feel your brain
bloom as your heart roars
to flame, an old stone
furnace smelting iron.

Awful to be able
to march on for months,
searching silent battlefields
in lockstep with ghosts,
injured by Minié balls
and folks with little myths.

Horrible to fall down
with your lame horse
and ambivalence, to know
as extremities drain that
lesser souls raise a toast,
faces glowing by the fire.

NOT XANADU

Tulip poplar turning leaves over in the breeze,
translucent mitts that know what it means to grow
when no one is looking. Ostensibly, every leaf
is a beginner, but that is enough to start

the bubbling that will blossom and surround
these leaves with color when the season breaks.
Azure means the blue of sky, an enormous idea

patched through. Forget me not: blue water,
blue breath, bluebells along roadsides,
dogs rolling in blue mysteries. So, no,
this is not Xanadu, but here there is the blue.

10% GHAZAL

Solar eclipse, August 21, 2017

What I could do with only 10% of the sun.
Write my first initial in the sky.

With 10% of you, I could work for ninety.
Write my initial backward in the sky.

Ten ants out of a hundred decided to march
up the back of my shirt.

10% of you might bring down an empire.
10% might change anything you want to change.

What I could do with only 10% of your attention.
Write my initial upside down in the sky.

Only one bee flew up my skirt
and left me professing its power.

10% of the light is more than I can see directly.
10% makes the day shine almost as bright.

BREAK ME WITH KISSES

The bruises of love turn yellow and green.
I bit in a moment's intensity.

Happiness, if one can account for times
like these in terms like this, might be reason

enough to rake my teeth across your blush
leaving my mark. Oh, surface everywhere—

and what it cannot tell. I thought I knew
your tributaries and rivers as mine,

our shoal one finning unified body.
Please teach me your secret continental

divides and organize my lessons, for
I am slow and require repetitions.

Inevitable, our drifting beyond
dragons, both of us mapping this ocean.

SAMSON, REVERSED

In the lion Samson slayed,
a honeycomb buzzed.
He ate bees with his honey.

LITTLE NOVEL

1.
Eyes lock as he walks
across the street. You have not yet met
your destiny, Child.

2.
A number of things intervene, pulling
you asunder until you dare date him.

You find out he's also seeing...

He pulls out
a moment too late, and the rabbit hops.

3.
It was always your decision,
alone, to make.

4.
Memory serves up repercussions.

He contacts you after ten years
of wearing a beard, he says.

You cannot open the file
to see his face. He says, "To you,

the years have been kind."

5.
Open ending with a period.

MISDIRECTION

after Hieronymus Bosch's "The Conjurer"

Useless glasses perched on his nose,
the thief gazes skyward throwing shade
as he grabs the dangling purse.

The globe window above his head
tilts in a seasonal nod to what's
at stake in this entertaining scene,

which is a window into being.
Distracted by the trick, the magician's
sleight of hand and all trinkets

of this magic show below the heavens,
our minds are slower
than the danger of such cunning,

targeting us as marks, blunting
our better natures, stealing us blind.
Caught in sphere and circle,

crowned by ridiculous hats,
we think everything is on the table,
the cups, the glistening marbles,

even the magic wand, and something
like a frog about to leap—
our rapt attention meets an owl,

our own lost wisdom, peering.
The boy we once were
watches us with fascination,

but the crowd is busy looking askance.
Devil's ears twitch on the dog
below the table where our eyes do not reach.

We're trained on the decoy,
the golden ball that trips us into losing
every god we ever wanted to behold.

SOME BONES FROM JOHN THE BAPTIST

Designed to hold the Baptist's bones,
this empty gold monstrance

lost its jewels to Napoleon
on his way to steal the Rosetta stone.

On islands, someone must leave or return—
in the fourteenth century

the last Grand Master fled Malta, packing
relics of St. John. The Baptist's wrist

and arm bones proved poor omens:
in Paris, Jacques de Molay was burned.

On this rock a month, I've waded
long lines to tour the Grand Master's Palace;

bright armor and weaponry intrigue me
less than this vessel's emptiness.

By the ninth century, St. John's bones had
traversed east to west, Antioch to Constantinople.

Gifted to the abbey of Citreaux, they paused in France,
before moving on to the Knights Hospitallers

of Jerusalem and Rhodes, thence the relics' arrival
in Valletta, at St. John's red cross of Malta.

Like Byron, I won't be sorry to leave heraldry
and endless bells pealing in my wake.   >

When I thought my return ticket to Rome canceled,
I fell to my knees in supplications.

In St. John's Co-Cathedral, I stand before
Caravaggio's dying prophet, angel, forerunner,

first cousin who greeted the Lord womb to womb,
whose father was struck dumb, tongue

only loosed at his birth. An ornate platter
awaits the saint's thought matter,

his scarlet garment as garish
as the blood seeped from his throat.

It's 2009, and I doubt many things
about myself, but in this moment, I behold

until I'm scuttled out by a guard, though
the velvet ropes corral no other tourists.

In all my travels, waters of seas in which
I've splashed have entered my cells, exchanging,

yet there is only one place each person finally rests:
I've never proved proof to myself.

I think about taking a year to walk
the labyrinth of scattered bones.

In 2010, on a speck off the Bulgarian coast,
a marble altar box yields fragments

of the Baptist's skull, jaw, arm, and tooth.
His head turns up in Munich, a hand

in Montenegro, a portion in Egypt, too.
After de Molay met his stake,

the saint's translation did not slack.
Back to the Ottomans John's right arm flew

to a reliquary commissioned by Knights,
where now it waves from deep time's flight.

RUNNER, SWEATING

1.
Trucks from both directions
blocking,

      I dodge up and back
before crossing

         to the wrong side.

2.
To the boy in blonde dreads on the porch,
half hidden, I say,

        "Good morning."

        "Good morning," he says,
        "I like your shoes!"

3.
The old gray tabby with runny eyes
has not yet budged.

Neither frost, rain, nor my trudging
doth disturb the fur bunch.

4.
On the bridge, white woman
with buttocks of a bull,
ears synched to sounds I cannot hear.

Solemn Asian dad lurching ahead,
mom behind him, sunny,
daughter wrinkle-browed.

5.
Brown man in bright blue headphones
paused at the gas pumps,
speaking into his mic,

"Something about the way
you smiled at him,
or the way he looked at you."

6.
Running, running, I measure
lopes to a mere three miles,

my sweat linking dissimilarities.

My only fluidity = humidity;
humility maintains pleasure in equalities.

UNDER THE MOUNTAIN

The copper beech replaced the copper beech.
You spot only the second not the first.
A plethora of replacements awaits your eye.
You never know what you are seeing.

A horseman rides by the tree. He doesn't spy
the original or the second, only the branch
of the third. Horses exist on apples in the hand
not the blind fruit fallen over time.

Aromatic circumstance of cinnamon and juniper—
you want what you want when you want it
not a moment before or after. Wait for the third
brush, remember the second and the first.

MR. LIBERTY: CENTO FOR THE PEOPLE

June 5, 1788, Virginia Convention

That government is, or ought to be, instituted for the common benefit, protection, and security of the people, nation or community;....and that, whenever any government shall be found inadequate or contrary to these purposes, a majority of the community hath an indubitable, unalienable, and indefeasible right to reform, alter or abolish it...

—Article three of the Virginia Declaration of Rights

THIS, sir, is the language of democracy—

But how different is the genius
of your new Constitution from this!

Your president may easily become king....
Where are your checks in this government?

Your strongholds will be in the hands of your
enemies. Show me that age and country where

the rights and liberties of the people were placed
on the sole chance of their rulers being good

men without a consequent loss of liberty! If
your American chief be a man of ambition

how easy is it for him to render himself absolute!
The president, in the field, at the head of his army,

can prescribe the terms on which he shall reign
master, so far that it will puzzle any American

ever to get his neck from under the galling
yoke. If ever he violate the laws...if he be guilty,

will not the recollection of his crimes teach him
to make one bold push for the American throne?

What will then become of you and your rights?

EVERYTHING, INCLUDING THE BONES

I'm letting this stale chicken go, after
stashing it in the freezer for trash day.

I'm dropping my guard, emptying
my hands. I offer you no weapon.

My clean hands are most likely
cold. My circulation suffers

when I'm crying or afraid.
I have trouble holding it together.

I'm holding out my hand. Into
this Big Blue, a few days ago,

I shoved a lot of walnuts husked in green,
and you know they're heavy as sin

and probably as complicated, maybe
in the end more so than I ever

dreamed. Don't get me started,
and don't gloss me over. I've been

here for a while, and you've been
sneaking around. You even dropped

your stuff into my recycling bin! How
could you? I've got your number,

so I called. I said, "Is this your
giant pile of marketing material, your

stack of outdated consumer maps, your
three 30lb bundles?" You hesitated.

I wondered if you'd claim your shit.
Finally, you said, "Yes. I dumped them."

And I said, "Well, come and get it!"

WHAT FALLS

In the morning, I could already hear my downspouts clattering like bumbling skunks, the likes of which had been a midnight plague up until the rains came chasing Pepé's cousins under the half-finished porch next door. One night I'd heard a certain thump followed by a screech or merely a fierce squeak, and then a pungent waft slammed me back onto my pillows. Oh boy, it was bad, and set me to wondering how long its plume would last, how enveloping it might become, when the fumes subsided or crested their wave, at least growing no worse, and the realization crashed over me that perhaps the skunk had sprayed next door, and what I'd just been treated to was a shifting of the winds. Not so with freezing rain, however, which fell everywhere at once. Barking dogs could not chase it away. Nothing about this weather would end for me, until everyone in town was no longer dripping wet, if not exactly dry again.

RUNNER, REVERSED

Screeching rail cars, ties crossed and pounded,
moon halved and canted over the sign
of an electric company founded

in 1913. Where is the boy whose head
I cradled in my lap sometime in the 1970s—
a romantic gesture instead

of holding hands—whose dark curls smelled
of cigarettes toked by adults and faintly
of earwax as he compelled

me to silence and recounted unbidden
that he had seen his mother shot dead
after she had been beaten

by his father, who then shot himself in the head?
Age two, waiting in the doorway, he
had no trouble, way past time for bed,

remembering every detail. I couldn't move
my legs beneath his mind that held
two violent deaths and proved

my experience was limited to a ranting
self-dramatizing dad. Dark-haired boy
no longer cried about much of anything,

repeating his imprints in dull tones.
I pictured his house thicker than water
razed to rubble and stifled moans.

The coal cars are searching for a place,
piling up many engines, pulling together
toward a bend where all things trace

a path and pass on shining multiple tracks.
Last of October's fireflies hover the grasses.
I wanted to run home afterward and act

as normal as possible at the table
of Mother's perfectly balanced meal:
one meat, a starch, and two vegetables.

WHERE WATERS MEET

Where South China Sea merges Pacific,
we watch ridges of current rippling
nearly into flame as one pair of wings
entangles another, as one body
of water seizes its brother confined
in a sack of time. Grab my hand and gaze
over dangerous cliffs into whitecaps.
Earth is one organism, with humans

not the whole planet, but neither are we
nothing. I awaken each night hearing
or remembering metallic couplings,
coal cars and engines grasping hands of steel
far away from a meeting of oceans,
with you flung far from the music of trains.

REPRISE

Seedling starter and hoe-the-row gardener,
faithless planter of blueberry bushes
that yet sprout and yield. Inheritor
of the green thumb and a righteous chorus

of seasonal cues. Dawn's coffee cup roamer,
measurer of beloved, blue Miracle-Gro—
in earthworms and compost-scent delighter.
It was in spring, remember, when psychosis

tipped its straw hat, and the farmer/father
tilled ground zero of paranoias:
squash, cucumber, green bean accuser,
left shoulder hitched and bickering brows,

wife and daughters' most vexing confuser.
Different birds sing and raise clutches.
Behold, the old is passed away forever.
Memory sprouts chicory and clover.

TREE FROGS

Night swimmers check pool
skimmers into which speckled
frogs have sucked, bunched up

green packages of
live matter without trumpets.
We stand by for jumps.

One ancient bullfrog,
front leg pinned by saltwater
and dissolving, waits

for rescue. We can't
save anything from ourselves,
not even barking

tree frogs. All our frogs
are barking frogs, our needs our
own. Don't make me leave

this one world, please don't.

SPARROW, REVERSED

I looked for my sparrow all
night, wild hopeless night.
Tucked in the canvas awning,

head bowed away, white-splattered
tail turned toward me,
my sparrow, yet never mine.

RIVER SCHOOL

Admit me to the school of skittering
minnows and the raw skin of the sycamore

where silent, water-light movies play
beneath the leaves and limbs.

Admit me, legacy of the Alleghanian
orogeny with mountain origins,

to your twenty-four species of fishes,
especially the mottled sculpin,

fantail darter, wild rainbow and
brown. And in your highest tributaries,

above 1,000 feet, where temperatures
never reach seventy, the painterly

native brook trout, spotted spawning
mid-October, swifting deep karst pools

hemlock shadowed. Tiny shells
depositing oceanic spells bobble just

beyond my reach on the riffle bed
that reflects full branches in the heat.

Rowdy dragonflies raft an oak leaf,
their fraternity whirls past as I drift.

Admit me to the rites of the inner
tube and the privileges of being dunked

onto a ripple of rocks and hung up
in sunken trunks, ensnared by rooted fingers

of embankment. I float here knowing
that so much of this river's invisible,

as is love and all that means
anything to us, running underground

through limestone, coring caves,
firing synapses with a water mind

only to rise at Coursey Springs.
The green heron has been listening

from its high nest at the bend, as we
waddle like upside-down terrapins,

paddling finny hands and legs
in the currents of 300 million years.

ACKNOWLEDGMENTS

I offer my sincere thanks to several generous readers—Jeanne Larsen, Carol Moldaw, Dara Wier, Robert Schultz, and Angela Ball—and to the editors of the following journals and anthologies in which some of these poems first appeared:

A Literary Guide to Southern Appalachia, Street and McLarney, eds., University of Georgia Press, 2019: "Four-Chambered Heart."

Artemis 2020: "River School."

California Quarterly: "Sparrow, Reversed"

Crosswinds Poetry Journal

FictionFix (poetryfix): "If I am Wrong," "Considering the Alternative," "It Must Be."

ISLE: Interdisciplinary Studies in Literature and Environment: "Roanoke Logperch."

jubilat: "Everything Including the Bones."

JuxtaProse: "Not Xanadu."

New World Writing: "Misdirection."

O. Henry: The Art & Soul of Greensboro; and *Salt: The Art & Soul of Wilmington*: "Dear Sylvia."

Poems in the Waiting Room, 5.1 & as a broadside published by Carilion Clinics: "10% Ghazal."

The American Journal of Poetry: "Everyman" (as "He Was"), "Under the Mountain," "Transmogrify."

The Cast-Iron Airplane that Can Actually Fly: Contemporary Poets Comment on Their Prose Poems, Peter Johnson, ed., MadHat Press, 2019: "What Falls."

The Punch Magazine (thepunchmagazine.com; World Poetry/Prose Portfolio): "Cinquain Sonnets," "Reverie," "What's Cooking," "Can you Draw out a Leviathan with a Fishhook?" "Reversed Samson," "Some Bones from John the Baptist."

A very few notes:

Not Xanadu alludes to "Kubla Khan" by Samuel Taylor Coleridge, the first lines of which read, *In Xanadu did Kubla Khan/ A stately pleasure dome decree.*

"Psalm Birds" borrows lines from Psalm 102.

Patrick Henry's speech known as "Give me Liberty or Give me Death," delivered March 23, 1775, was reconstructed by William Wirt and first published in *Sketches of the Life and Character of Patrick Henry* (1817).

"Liberty or Empire," delivered by Patrick Henry, June 5, 1788, is recorded in the proceedings from the Convention of Virginia. The complete text can be found here: https://archive.org/details/debatesotherproc00virg/page/46

"My Mistress' eyes are nothing like the sun" is the first line of Shakespeare's sonnet 130.

"Onion Story" appears to be in conversation with Adrienne Rich's "Peeling Onions." I don't recall having read Rich's poem before writing mine, but this is no matter; the poems are in conversation, just as Ibsen's *Peer Gynt* stirred us both.

ABOUT THE AUTHOR

Cathryn Hankla is a native of southwest Virginia and the author of fifteen books, including *Fortune Teller Miracle Fish*, *Galaxies*, and *Lost Places: On Losing and Finding Home*. *Not Xanadu* is her tenth poetry collection. Her work has been awarded a Virginia Commission for the Arts grant, a PEN syndicated fiction prize, and the James Boatwright poetry prize, among other honors, and has appeared in numerous journals and anthologies. Her university career spans four decades: at Hollins University she directed the Jackson Center for Creative Writing, chaired her department, and continues to serve as poetry editor of *The Hollins Critic*; visiting appointments include Washington & Lee University, University of Virginia, and Randolph College (formally Randolph Macon Women's College). She exhibits her visual art at Market Gallery in Roanoke, Virginia, where she makes her home, and offers writing and strategic communication consultations.